MAGIC AND OTHER REALISM

Library of Congress Cataloging in Publication Data

Main entry under title:

Magic and Other Realism

(Library of American Illustration) (Visual communication books)
1. Illustration of books—20th century—United States.
2. Magic realism (Art)—United States. 3. Realism in
art—United States. I. Munce, Howard. II. Society of
Illustrators, New York. III. Series.
NC975.M33   1979   759.13   79-18013

ISBN 0-8038-4721-1

Published simultaneously in Canada by
Saunders of Toronto, Ltd., Don Mills, Ontario

Printed in the United States of America

Society of Illustrators Library of American Illustration

MAGIC AND OTHER REALISM

The Art of Illusion

VISUAL COMMUNICATION BOOKS

Hastings House, Publishers
10 East 40th Street, New York 10016

For The Society of Illustrators
Howard Munce, *Editor*
Robert Hallock, *Designer*
Gerald McConnell, *Co-ordinator*

CONTENTS

ROBERT GEISSMANN

TO GEISSMANN—WITH HIGHEST REGARD

This book is dedicated to Robert Geissmann who first planned it and was designated to be its designer.

His fatal illness interrupted.

Realism is what Bob zealously practiced when he moved from lettering to illustration long ago.

Many examples of his excellent work can be found in past *Art Directors'* and *Illustrators' Annuals* — often as an award winner. His writings and some of his last works are found here.

What can't be found, unfortunately, is a replacement for himself: he was a congenital organizer. This quality continually made the Society of Illustrators a better and more professional place. He was an outstanding President for two terms He was an outstanding friend for all terms. And he possessed a bounce and spark and sense of fun that disappeared when he did. Unfortunately, you can take it with you.

HOWARD MUNCE

THREE DAY PASS IN PARIS
Courtesy of the United States Air Force Collection

REALISM BY DESIGN

The marriage of painting and design is not just a marriage of convenience. It is, in my opinion, a marriage of necessity. If we were to pursue this analogy further, we might say that painting is the mother, and design the father. This artistic liaison, taken lightly, has often produced bastard compositions!

I have admired the technique and skills of many artists whose sense of design (composition) left much to be desired. It should be stated that in this discussion I will use the terms "design" and "composition" interchangeably. If in some usages there is a difference, we might assume that composition always implies the total painting, while design might relate to specific segments thereof.

In pondering design in painting, I found it helpful to glance back through some of my art books. All the great painters had an instinctive (or was it learned?) sense of design, but some were so outstanding in this area that they should be mentioned. Piero della Francesca, of the Umbrian school, in *The Battle of Constantine* dramatically demonstrates what I am talking about. Not only is the total painting a masterpiece of design, but I have seen it masked into twelve different areas, each of which was also a gem of design. Another example — painted some two hundred years later and curiously reminiscent of it — is *The Surrender of Breda* by Valasquez.

Closer to our own time (and my own inclinations in subject matter) is the famous American William Harnett, one of the masters of *trompe l'oeil*. His paintings are composed of many theme elements seemingly casually arranged but actually done with consummate design sense.

Composition is made up of four major elements: total area of the picture, depth, line and value. In abstract painting, which incidentally does need the element of depth, the design concept is usually more easily recognized, whereas in realistic painting this factor is often not immediately recognized because we are involved in actual things. Our eye is brought into the depth of the picture, the lines tend to control the eyes' movement from area to area, and most important the values (and color) contribute to the total design.

It has been said that the picture starts in the mind. It therefore may seem heretical in the context of this article to state that I will often approach a painting with a "master concept" only as to subject matter. The design emerges as I add the elements necessary to carry the theme of the work.

Parenthetically, it would be obvious from a quick perusal of my paintings that it is seldom possible to bring all the elements together so that I may "paint from life". Most are done from a collection of research. Backgrounds usually come from photographs taken on my travels here and abroad. Whenever possible, I set up a still life composition of all available articles in my studio, while other objects must be drawn in their appropriate places from my file and other sources. It is such a boon to have the objects right in front of you and see the colors and shadows from one to another. This usually necessary procedure of multiple research sources leads to many challenges for the realistic painter. The problems of divergent eye levels, unknown size relationships, and contradictory light sources must all be resolved.

It has seemed to me that the painter of realism who has a talent for design has an advantage over the pure craftsman since he can instinctively solve the problems of composition and then put his creativity into the areas of meaningful and realistic symbols which can take the painting beyond the ordinary.

Most people are interested in the content of a painting, but a well-designed painting can add a sense of order and involvement whether or not one realizes how this came about.

From *North Light*, Published by Fletcher Art Services, Inc.

ROBERT GEISSMANN

FOREWORD

Realism is the precise delineation of actual objects in an attempt to define their intrinsic significance. The resulting painting may make a poetic or romantic statement, or may simply be a technical tour de force to fool the eye (*trompe l'oeil*). The optical realism is achieved by our eyes binocularly giving volume to the objects observed. The nearer the object the sharper and larger it becomes. On the flat surface of a painting, depth must thus be achieved by illusion. Of course, the ultimate test of any work of art is the relationship of the elements to each other. They must all be vital and functional to the whole composition.

From the beginning of time man has sought for reality. Prehistoric cave paintings captured the elusive action of animals, his real world of survival. There has been a kind of black magic associated with the creation of illusion. The evolution of the rules of perspective and tonality and the refinement of techniques resulted in the high point of the Renaissance. The ultimate objective was to remove all traces of how it was done in order to create an unchallenged image of what it appeared to be.

Magic realism has often been referred to as romantic reality. The "magic" is simply the artist's ability to cast out, from the hundreds of impressions that flash through his brain and before his eyes, all but the most essential, and then to render these objects with such skilled and meticulous techniques as to convince the observer of the utter truth of his rendition of his reality. This can be carried, of course, a step further—as with a Magritte — into Surrealism. For instance, the scene may be realistically painted but given an ambiguous and metamorphic relationship. It is placing realistic objects in an unfamiliar context. Gravity can be defied, as well as familiar size relations. Fact becomes fiction.

This book is not a historical review of realism, but presents the work of contemporary illustrators' application to the subject.

ROBERT HALLOCK

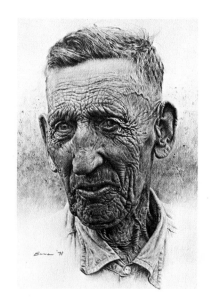

This book gives me a great opportunity to try and explain the nature of my work. While many frown upon the use of photography in fine art and illustration, it has been used by artists since its invention. It is merely a tool, and enables one to conceive situations previously impossible to execute.

I had always wanted to do good realism and was trained for it. I spent several years working from the model, eight hours a day. We did color charts, composition and illustration problems. We learned to rent costumes, hire top models, do our own photography. I had admired the fine realism of Rockwell, Crockwell, Cornwell and Leyendecker, not realizing that they too used these aids. I thought they had a magic that I never would have.

I have observed that most still life paintings and portraiture had, for centuries, been done in a traditional manner—mostly indoors with the light from a window or skylight. Outdoors situations were posed indoors, be it hot or cold. I once waited for the snow to fall just right on an old saddle. After several windy, clumpy snows it fell one night — gentle and fine. But it was 20° below zero! I wanted it in soft light before sunrise. It would have been impossible to paint from nature. Because of the detailed execution, my paintings take a long time to do. I like to capture attitudes and often do outdoor situations. You could never get a model to pose for days in the cold and have the same soft gray-day light. The wind also does subtle things with hair and clothes that would be hard to fake. High-speed action situations become possible. All this has nothing to do with being a good artist, but it sure helps.

The illustrator must do a great variety of subjects that must be technically correct and aesthetically satisfying. It could be when heat control was invented for the Linotype machine, animals in motion or a winter scene assigned in July. Even the greats, Rembrandt and Rubens, had trouble doing horses in action. The camera can stop the motion and let us observe positioning of the legs.

For many years the magazines were filled with artwork for both ads and stories. Then, some 20 years ago, fast film was developed. This enabled photographers to almost make the illustrator extinct. They created a quality of realism that the average reader could relate to. Much illustration was no longer convincing.

However, many situations could not be photographed, such as winter scenes in summer or ones that would involve exorbitant costs. So, because I can do very convincing realism, my career flourished. I could do historical situations from black and white reference and do them in color with a convincing quality.

The photograph as reference can only do so much. It basically has hard edges and distorts proportions.

The knowledge I obtained in art school and practice has enabled me to cope with the changes in illustration and compete with the photographer and often surpass him.

JAMES E. BAMA

Born: New York City
Studied: High School of Music & Art, Art Students League, Frank Reilly
Clients: *Saturday Evening Post, Reader's Digest, Argosy*, leading paperbacks, Ford, Coca Cola, General Electric, Fuller Brush, Penn. RR, Schaefer Beer, etc.
Exhibited: Society of Illustrators, McCulley Gallery, Carson Gallery, Hammer Galleries, Husberg Gallery, Cowboy Hall of Fame

13

14

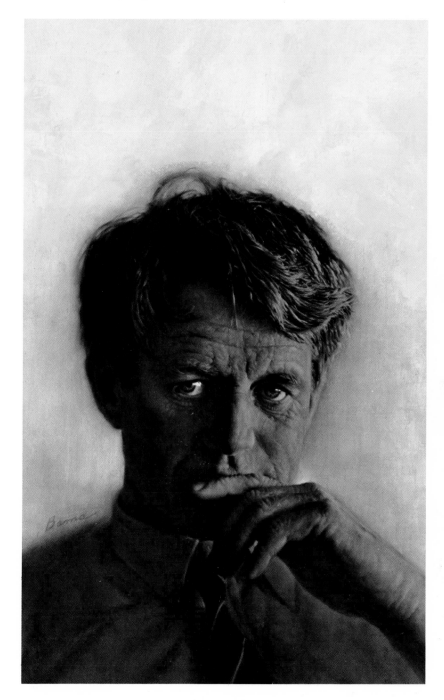

JOHN C. BERKEY

Born: Edglen, N.D.
Clients: Texaco, Warner, Otis Elevator, U.S. Steel, *Sports Afield*, Paramount, 20th Century Fox, Dell Publishers, Doubleday, Ballantine, Fawcett, Avon, Warner Communications

Realism is a word of varied meanings — some related to looking at paintings rather than painting them.

To me realism has to do with a definition of space, plus the light within the space accurately interpreted. I think of realism in painting first as painting light. It becomes the basis of the solution to the problems of form and space within the picture.

Much of the commercial work I have done has been in one of two areas: future-space and historical pictures. My preliminary work begins with a series of sketches. They are simple-to-abstract shapes that suggest the final subject. These help me establish what I would like to see and from where.

In advertising work, the view is often critical because of what must be seen. In fantasy it's usually a combination of the two. Shapes, speed and space are exaggerated in sketches.

I generally make small color schemes in tempera looking for an interesting light source and color combinations for the finished painting. I work seated and resolve the problem of being on top of the work with two mirrors: one reflects to a second one that I can see as I work. This allows me to see the piece from about eight feet without moving. It's easier to see the space within the picture this way. Also, shapes are evident from distance not detectable close up.

The sketches are an easy way for a client to see my final intent. The first printed material for *King Kong* was a sketch — the final painting a year later!

Every picture presents different problems, all of the suggested realism in the sketches has to be sharply defined. Reference on most subjects is in my own files. Often reference data explains the surface of a subject but my painting involves its reason.

Science fiction art is enjoyable since there isn't a right or wrong idea to resolve. It's conjectural.

My paintings are usually done in tempera. I mix my own paint and mediums and vary their characteristics depending on the subject. The drying time is variable and affects the look of a piece. Problems of color change from wet to dry can be controlled.

I start with an underpainting and continue into details, adjusting as one part affects another. When I consider the light contrasts stable I may spray the color underpainting with a glaze of half black and the allover shadow color. It then involves painting the light — rather than light *and* shadow.

I rarely work from models of any kind. I prefer making drawings based on my sketches. We must first see where we are in that painting. It motivates our judgements about what we see. Is it believable?

We cannot paint the sound of a bird singing in a tree. Realism is the illusion of that space where a bird sings — and the song is part of our vision.

17

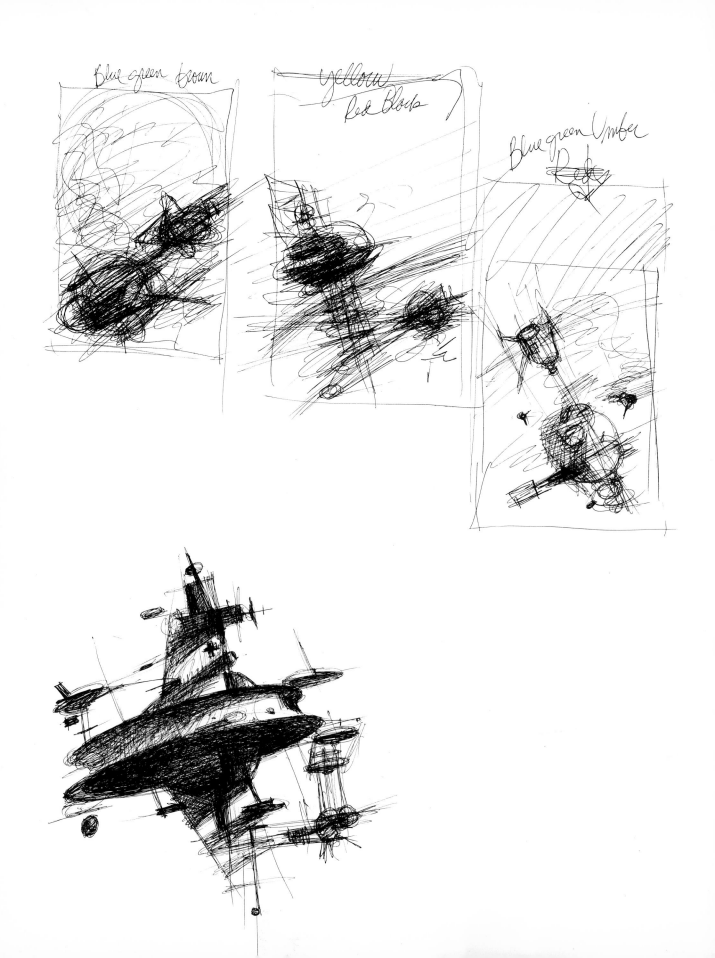

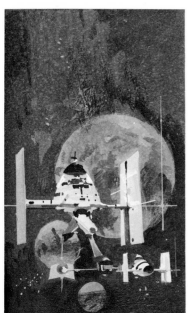

19

THE INSIDE JOKE. *Collection: Mrs. Elizabeth Sparacio*

Some people call it magic realism, some call it Surrealism, some — with adept tongues or pens — call it *trompe l'oeil*. When cornered, I describe my work as a hard-boiled kind of still life painting.

Of course I believe there is in my painting something more than what seems apparent to the eye. What can be

AARON BOHROD

Born: Chicago
Studied: Crane Jr. College, Chicago Art Institute, Art Students League, John Sloan
Clients: *Life* (artist war correspondent), *Time* (covers), *Look*
Exhibited: Extensively
Awards: Carr Landscape Prize; 7 Art Institute of Chicago Awards, 2 Guggenheim Fellowships; S.F. Golden Gate Exhibition; Carnegie Int'l; Calif. Watercolor Soc.; Penn. Acad. of Fine Arts; Artists for Victory—Metropolitan Museum, Clark Prize & Silver Medal—Corcoran; National Academician, Saltus Gold Medal—N.A., Childe Hassam Purchase Prize—N.A.; Kirk Memorial Prize—N.A., Wisconsin Governor's Award
Member: National Academy of Design
Teaching: Chicago Art Inst. '38, So. Ill. Univ. '42-'43, No. Mich. Univ. '52, Artist in Residence Univ. of Wis. '48-'73

seen is an intense realization of three dimensional objective form.

But the reasons for the particular choices of objects in my compositions and their arrangement lie in the direction of symbolic expression: a literary allusion, the pictorial telling of a small joke — or in rare cases — a profound truth; the pointing up of conventional or unconventional similarities and disparities. These are not the principal reasons, however, for my engaging in a form of work which is peculiarly demanding; a form which is painfully slow to evolve and a kind of work which puts me at an economic disadvantage with those who have devised ways of expression which flow quickly and readily from one's hand. What is most exhilarating is the work itself: the "they can't take *that* away from me" reward of having brought to intense visual life a collection of fragments of the world; the poor artist's equivalent of Blake's seeing all eternity in a grain of sand.

Recently a New York art dealer viewed (without favor) some of the paintings in my studio and asked me whether I was aware that most of the objects I chose for use in my paintings could only be classified as *kitsch*. I had never thought to differentiate between the intrinsically beautiful and the authentic antique object (though I have no antipathy to their use) and the mostly ordinary, sometimes clumsily put together reflections of man's cultural endeavors. I feel I may comment on all physical matter whether it be a flourishing or decaying product of nature or whether it is the echo of an old master painting, an innately admirable work of art or of worthy craftsmanship, or the flawed, commercial and sometimes tasteless things man has been known to make. I would like to think that all of nature's work and all man-made things can be equal subjects for my brush.

In the beginning I may have a theme in mind. A search ensues to collect from my shelves or from any conceivable source the objects I must put together to serve as models for the visual translation of that theme. Or, a viewing of the already established sea of collected materials along with, perhaps, the acquisition of a new object or two will evoke a thought that will serve as the idea for a painting.

The objects, wherever possible, are mounted in a three dimensional mockup with flexible allowance for enlargement or reduction of scale.

The surface I work on is a smooth-as-glass gesso panel. My palette is as extensive as I can safely make it. My medium is one part sun-thickened linseed oil to three and one half parts of turpentine. My method is first to paint thinly and tentatively with my diluted oils followed by a wave-after-wave attack for form development and refinement until the weeks of necessary application result in a completed work.

21

A BROWN STUDY. *Collection: Dr. & Mrs. Craig Aswegan*

INNER AND OUTER WOMAN. *Collection: Mr. & Mrs. James Devlin*

THE HIERONIMUS DETAIL. *Collection: Dr. & Mrs. George C. Wussow*

STANLEY BORACK

Born: New York City
Studied: High School of Music & Art, Art Students League, Frank Reilly
Clients: Movie posters, advertising, record albums, paperback covers and various other publications
Exhibited: Grand Central Art Galleries, Society of Illustrators
Member: Grand Central Art Galleries, Society of Illustrators

To my way of thinking, realistic painting is the highest form of painting. It takes more time and patience than any other. It requires the epitome of craftsmanship.

For the book illustration pictured here, the type layout was designed first and the remaining space was left for the illustration. The painting had to tell the story of the hero's life and the important characters in the book. The approach had to have a "big book" look.

Research was needed for the resort, the tent, and the New York skyline. It was necessary to dress the hero in black and pull him forward in the illustration to focus the reader's attention.

The sketch I submitted went through some minor changes in costume and the gestures of the characters. The skyline had to be more monumental.

I used the same models for various characters and made use of other photographic heads that I had on file.

For the finish I used a 20 × 30 Morilla board. I like its texture. I added more palm trees to improve the design.

In painting this illustration, I proceeded from left to right. Some illustrators don't like this approach and like to lay in the whole thing as a first stage to get a "look". I work as I do because I see the entire painting finished in my mind and I have my sketch to guide me.

I mostly use small Winsor & Newton watercolor brushes. I find them excellent for heads, hands and small areas. Unfortunately turpentine shortens the life of a watercolor brush rather quickly. I usually buy them by the dozen so I'm never caught without one that behaves.

Painting this illustration went smoothly and was well received by Jim McIntyre, the art director.

25

PAUL CALLE

Easter 1972

Born: New York City
Studied: Pratt Institute
Clients: McCall's, Ladies' Home Journal, Time, Redbook,
    Saturday Evening Post, National Geographic, Reader's
    Digest, Time-Life
Exhibited: Smithsonian, National Gallery of Art, McCulley
    Fine Art, Husberg Fine Art
Awards: '51 Hamilton King Award, 2 Awards of Excellence
    (SI), Pratt Contemporary Achievement Medal, Franklin
    Mint Medal for Distinguished Western Painting
Member: Society of Illustrators

Often, artists spend so much time trying to imitate a current vogue, or create the "new image," that by the time they do so, it's old hat again. How much better it would be to try to express one's honest self!

Life is the subject material of an artist and all the experiences encountered become part of one's art. Creating a style is not something that one sets out to accomplish on purpose. It is something that evolves and grows with the maturing person. It is not a deliberate process, but evolutionary. Obviously, we're influenced by other artists along the way. This becomes input into our total being. When we find out who *we* are, then this process is well on the way to producing the true individual. Training is very important. However, the most important ingredient is drawing. It's through constant drawing that we develop.

I thoroughly enjoy making pictures. I consider myself fortunate in never having been stereotyped as to content. This has enabled me to experience the visual world as stimulus. Whether my paintings and drawings are destined for books, editorial art, advertising or galleries, the essential problems remain the same. One must visually articulate an idea or emotion in a pleasing and dramatic way. Always, the subject must be approached with enthusiasm for a real personal expression.

While the painter, employing his full palette of color, is acutely aware of the importance of a strong value relationship in his work, the graphic artist, with his limited range of black and white, realizes the importance of tonal relationships. To express oneself in the area of black and white pencil drawing, whether as a preliminary to a painting or as a finished piece, is to be intimately concerned with the control of these relationships. This should not only be appreciated, but regarded as vital to a successful composition. The proper exploitation sets and controls the mood of the composition together with the rhythm and design patterns.

In any drawing, it's immeasurably more important to convey the *feeling* of a subject, to *interpret* the characteristics of a tree, of a head, of a house than to render what is available to you with a camera. Quick impressions gathered by on the spot sketching are of greater value. Details can be filled in from photos.

My photography is done for future reference. The advantage is the real possibility of acquiring much more informality and detail than any drawing made on the spot. It serves as an additional source, a supplement to the mental image. The final work is a composite.

Art is aesthetically good or bad, regardless of the artist's procedure. My work is meaningless if it fails to stand alone and evoke a response from the viewer. That's what it should be—a visual experience.

Excerpts from THE PENCIL *by Paul Calle, published by Fletcher Art Services*

DON CROWLEY

Born: California
Studied: Art Center, L.A., Stanley Reckless, Harold Kramer
Clients: Major advertisers, books, magazines
Exhibited: Southwest Galleries, Tucson, Az.
Member: Society of Illustrators

When I received the assignment to design a painting depicting The Bill of Rights, my instructions were to produce a still life that would tell the story through the use of objects. It should have dignity befitting the subject. The technique should have a timeless quality and the finished work should be able to hold its own as a painting after its use as an illustration. William Harnett's work was mentioned as an example. There were no other directions or layout to follow and I was asked to submit a quarter size sketch for client approval within three to four weeks.

Step One was the research to discover who conceived and wrote The Bill of Rights and when they were adopted. This part of the job turned out to be very educational.

Step Two was the staging of the whole thing. After many thumbnail sketches I decided to borrow one of Harnett's devices of using a cupboard door with a protruding shelf on which to arrange my props. I built this myself and painted it an appropriate color.

Step Three was to find a central element to build around. After much searching I was fortunate enough to find an unusual eagle frame with openings for two portraits. It fit my space exactly. With this central piece determined, most of the other elements suggested themselves.

After the props were set in place and properly lit I took working photographs in black and white. The painting was done from the photos, rather than the setup itself, for two reasons: one, rented or borrowed props have to be returned quickly and, two, the objects in this case were not the proper color. I am always influenced by the presence of real things. The original eagle frame, for instance, was a sickly orange-gold. I wanted the blue-green of the background to dominate, so I prepared a large jar of this color and mixed some with each of the other colors as the painting progressed. The painting was done with Grumbacher oils on a gesso panel. I used a limited palette of white, lemon yellow, cadmium yellow deep, cadmium red, cerulean blue, ultramarine blue and black. The finished size is 16" × 21".

THE BILL OF RIGHTS

THE DECLARATION OF INDEPENDENCE

VETERAN'S DAY

CHRIS

CORNER SHELF

WILD TURKEY

KEN DAVIES

Born: New Bedford, Ma.
Studied: Yale School of Fine Art, Massachusetts School of Art, Boston
Clients: Wild Turkey Whiskey, Austin Nichols, Inc.
Exhibited: Work has been shown steadily in New York and New England Galleries and in dozens of National and European invitational exhibitions. Represented by Hirschl & Adler Galleries, N.Y.C.
Awards: Louis Comfort Tiffany Scholarship Grant, Purchase Prizes, Springfield Museum and Berkshire Museum, 2 Awards, Connecticut Academy of Fine Arts, 2 Awards, Silvermine Guild of Artists, Berkshire Art League, Meriden Art League, New Haven Arts Festival
Member: Connecticut Academy of Fine Arts, Silvermine Guild of Artists, New Haven Paint & Clay Club, Listed in "Whos Who in Art" and "Who's Who in the East", Society of Illustrators
Teaching: Dean, Paier School of Art, Hamden Ct.

My time is divided between studio painting and administrative duties at the Paier School of Art in Hamden, Conn. This is an ideal combination. In my studio, I paint *trompe l'oeil* compositions, still lifes, an occasional landscape. And every two or three years I do another bird for the Wild Turkey bourbon account.

This makes for a solitary life, but the time spent at the art school gives me a welcome change of pace. It prevents me from becoming a "studio hermit" and gets me out to meet new people, and perhaps keeps me from growing old. Daily contact with young enthusiastic art students allows me to remain at 32 (a milestone I reached 22 years ago when I decided it was enough).

In school I try to impress the students with the importance of a sound drawing, painting and design background. Once that is accomplished, I encourage them to get as "creative" as they can.

Back in the studio I try to practice what I preach. My own drawing, painting and perspective had better be right or I'll certainly hear about it from the students who are tougher critics than most art directors.

My still lifes are usually painted with the actual objects in front of me, but when this is not possible I photograph the subject from various angles, varying the lighting, and work from the slides. The finished paintings then go to my gallery—Hirschl & Adler.

For the first dozen years or so after I graduated from Yale Art School, I earned the bulk of my income painting situations for advertising. The only "commercial" work I do now are the Wild Turkey paintings. My relationships with both the agency (Nadler & Larimer) and the client (Austin, Nichols, Inc.) have always been most pleasant. One important reason is that I have always set my own deadlines—a rare luxury in the advertising world. Presently a sixth painting is in the works.

The backgrounds for these are done from slides. Over the years, I've accumulated hundreds of landscapes slides for reference and I can usually find what I need from them. The turkeys have been done from a combination of photographs, movies of the bird in action, mounted birds, personal observation and a generous sprinkling of idealization. Recently, I asked the agency to send me the material on wild turkeys from the New York Public Library picture file. When the package arrived, I was surprised to find several clippings of my own work.

These pictures are enjoyable to paint and are a pleasant change from my usual gallery work. It has been particularly gratifying that Austin, Nichols is pleased enough with the originals to have exhibited them in several fine art galleries around the country. There is only one disturbing fact about this account—I have to frequently admit that the most successful commercial painting I ever did was a "turkey"!

37

WINDOW ON DOCK STREET

THE BLACKBOARD

A SPOT OF RED

A

B

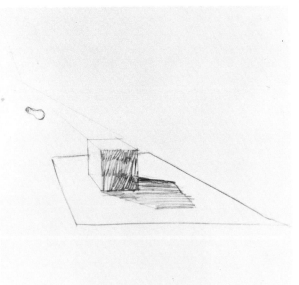

C

D

ROLAND J. DESCOMBES

Born: New York City
Studied: Art Students League, Frank Reilly School of Art.
Art Director of several major advertising agencies in New York and Europe before turning to illustration in 1970
Clients: United States Trust Co.; Time, Inc.; Simon & Schuster; Union Pacific; Doubleday
Member: Society of Illustrators

This particular piece (*fig. A*) was done to illustrate the history of a company that started out making seaplanes and follow its progress to the present where it is involved, among other things, in making components for nuclear submarines.

A description of the process used to complete this job is indicative of the way I work.

After the objective and direction had been established with the client, my first step was to decide on a basic design. The space to be used was a 11″ × 32″ format folded four times. The original layout was to have a progressive history illustrated across the lower third of the page with the type running across the upper two thirds. Trying to improve on this design, I took the shape that I was working with, very small, 1½″ × 4½″, and scribbled in the boxes (*fig. B*) until I got one that was pleasing and seemed right for this job.

The second step was to project onto tracing paper in several sizes all the objects that must appear to tell the story. I then began to arrange them (*fig. C*) into a design to fit into the original scribble as closely as possible.

This is the most exciting part of the job for me because this is where the piece is actually born. You realize the creation of a unique piece of art at this point and you have all the options to change and play with all the elements. Once this sketch is completed and approved by the client, the third stage, naturally, is the rendering of the final drawing.

Rather than discuss how I rendered this particular piece I believe it would be more instructive if I discussed the principle of the technique.

One of the stages of the sketch was to determine where the lights and darks would fall to give the best contrast to each of the elements within. In this case, using the darkness of the sea as a background into which lighter pictures have been placed. Next, the pencil lines are laid on planes (as the six sides of a cube, each side being a different plane) so infinitely more subtle are the planes on every object, and is the way in which every object is expressed in terms of light and shade.

The planes are rendered lighter or darker according to the light falling on it. The lightness or darkness is accomplished by using different grades of pencils and varying the white space between the pencil strokes. Each surface is rendered (*fig. D*) either by following the plane or the direction of light falling across it.

There are many subtleties such as highlights and reflections which are added as finishing touches and add a great deal to create the illusion of realism.

Simply stated this is how I create illusion. I believe that it is a sound drawing principal and works equally well when carried to the ultimate stage of color.

41

WHALING MEMORABILIA, *Courtesy Mystic Seaport Museum, Mystic, Conn.*

44

I would like to pay tribute to the Inanimate Objects that sit quietly in the studio and wait—that charge no model fees—can be rearranged and used over and over again and can even be eaten in a pinch.

Apart from the obvious choice of loaves of bread, fruits, seafood and other edibles, the still life artist's Selective Eye is always working—observing, sorting, evaluating, memorizing and acquiring objects and art-

STEVEN DOHANOS

Born: Lorain, Ohio
Studied: Cleveland School of Art
Clients: *Saturday Evening Post*; *Reader's Digest*; *Life*; *Medical Times*; has designed 21 U.S. postage stamps—is Chairman of the Postmaster General's Citizen Stamp Advisory Committee
Exhibited: Extensively
Awards: Elected to Hall of Fame by Society of Illustrators '71, Awards in both commercial and fine art fields
Member: Society of Illustrators, Dutch Treat Club
Teaching: Famous Schools (Founding Member)

ifacts to formalize into satisfactory compositions. A few of them will be isolated or placed in juxtaposition with others in a still life painting.

The objects will visually come alive on the canvas and be recreated two dimensionally and sometimes, hopefully, even achieve an illusion of *third dimension*. The artist attempts to recreate an illusion of believability—to make objects appear as real and lifelike with *magic realism* that it will "fool the eye".

The French have an expression for it—*trompe l'oeil* —a classic style of painting inanimate objects which can lend a special quality of art to the most prosaic of objects. There is showmanship involved in this form of still life painting because the artist involves the viewer in the game. One may even be tempted to *touch* the painting to find out if objects in it are third dimensional or just skillfully painted to look so.

I would emphasize that the selection of the objects should have significant relationship to one another. Each thereby contributes to the picture story. The collective design should have a meaning, a theme to the viewer and then logically given a title.

Now let me depart from the eclectic process and approaches used by the artist in searching for subject matter and reveal my lifelong love affair with "The Common Object."

All our lives are spent in acquiring, using and discarding things. In our relationship with them we develop attachments and nostalgic feelings. We find that the homely can be beautiful, the commonplace unusual.

As artists we each plan still life paintings in an individual way. We all react privately to signals we receive from objects found in nature or man-made.

Morandi, the great still life artist, was inspired by empty bottles of all shapes and sizes. He grouped them endlessly in arresting compositions of color.

For me the closest similar absorption with a common object has been my fascination with fire hydrants, a subject that has appeared repeatedly in my paintings. Sometimes in a supporting role in street scenes, but in most it is featured in lonely splendor revealing its form, color, its age and with the proximity of weeds, grass or small story-telling details to make it real.

I can savor a full painting experience with hydrants. No two are exactly alike. Their patina has a thousand variations and endless color combinations. Check it!

In the painting, *Whaling Memorabilia*, I tell the story of the romance and heritage of the industry at its peak. Against a backdrop of an early New England whaling town and harbor I arrange some handcrafted symbols that speak eloquently of those people who created them. Some were functional and some were ornamental. One thing is certain—they were all one of a kind— the common objects of their time.

45

48

DONALD E. DUBOWSKI

Born: St. Louis
Studied: Washington University School of Art, Frank
  Conway, Howard Jones, Siegfried Reinhardt
Clients: Hallmark Cards, Inc. (Design Director, Creative
  Services Div.)
Exhibited: City Museum, St. Louis; Temple Israel, St. Louis;
  Weatherspoon Art Gallery, N.C.; Society of Illustrators;
  Washington Univ., St. Louis; N.Y. World's Fair; Albrecht
  Gallery, St. Joseph, Mo.; Kansas City Art Inst.; Unitarian
  Gallery, K.C.; Nelson-Atkins Art Gallery, K.C.; Art
  Directors' Shows, K.C., traveling exhibition of Ten
  Missouri Painters. In numerous public and private
  collections.
Awards: Several
Teaching: Kansas City Art Institute '61-'65

The critical element in any illustration, and the one that most stimulates me, is its *purpose*. I don't have a lot of categorized solutions waiting for the right assignment to come along. Each one has its own character and purpose and demands that I illustrate according to its needs.

Certain intangibles are involved that cannot be specifically detailed into a formula to explain how an idea or a feeling is to be finally transformed.

There are two routes that I travel in my work—and these are the only constants. Sometimes I am exhilarated and everything falls into place. The idea, the execution and the little time it takes to solve a problem all seem almost too easy. Then there is the agony when nothing seems right. The idea isn't there, the drawing isn't right, the composition isn't good and the color feeling is terrible. The entire look seems forced. More thought, more consideration· of design and composition and *purpose* are pursued. I try simplification, redesigning, repainting—anything, to clarify the problem. Soon the mood changes and the illustration begins to work.

Although one illustration may flow effortlessly from mind to paper while another may be forced, I value both experiences. In each instance the illustration process is at work. What makes it challenging is that the outcome is seldom predictable until I actually get into it. Then I begin to visualize, think through possibilities, and start to work.

My subjects are nature and people. Beauty, life, rebirth are my themes. Situations that I have seen or experienced, some moment that I find stunning in its beauty, the abstract pattern of light and shadow, moments of solitude, landscapes filled with light—this is the kind of inspiration I need—the changing seasons. another generation of wildlife, a seagull soaring, a sunrise scene, a patch of field with snow melting off, a young person under a tree with a guitar and sunlight streaming through the tree.

When I determine the *purpose* of the illustration, I then use the writer's words and my images to make it an expression of the mood of our collective efforts. I don't believe in getting too comfortable in any one approach. Nor do I have a limitation on subjects to illustrate. All my work, however, is based upon detailed and meticulously developed drawing and composition. First to visualize, and then feel an affinity with what I see, is critical to the end result. The mood, composition, drawing, color, technique and medium are the elements which follow one another to completion.

I am after a variety of solutions to a variety of assignments. To bring surprise into each by searching for new visual approaches or interpretations is meaningful and, I hope comes through in my illustrations.

49

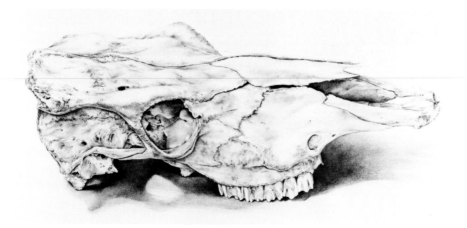

RICHARD FISH

Born: Philadelphia
Studied: University of Pennsylvania; Philadelphia College of
  Art; Ezio Martinelli; Frederick Gill; Raymond Ballinger
Clients: Volkswagen's *Small World*; Chatham Press;
  Random House; Atlantic-Little Brown; *Reader's Digest*,
  ICI America, Dravo Review; RCA
Exhibited: Kenmore Gallery; Munson Gallery; Butler
  Institute of American Art; Delaware Art Museum; Norfolk
  Museum, Philadelphia; Art Directors Shows; Society of
  Illustrators
Awards: Philadelphia Art Directors, Pennational Arts
  Annual
Member: Philadelphia Print Club

My taste for the old, the weatherstained and the ne-
glected was whetted and sharpened in territory closer
to home and more accessible — Cape Cod. But now I
have found another place ripe and rich with the past,
one that amply satisfies my desire to capture the flavor
of time gone by. This other echo of time is heard on the
western coasts of Scotland.

My tailor and I are thinking of applying for a patent
on my specially-pocketed sketching jacket. All that I
can't accommodate in an old gas mask bag, I tuck
neatly into pockets, all sizes, all shapes, on the inside
and outside of a warm, lightweight waterproof jacket.
Now I'm ready for another day's wandering through the
hills and glens.

The VW like my waterproof jacket, also seems tai-
lored to the sharply-turning, single-lane roads and the
steep grades. Anything larger would be incongruous.
"Wellingtons," binoculars, bird books, watercolors and
a dress-up jacket for hotel dining are in the back seat.
And there are also my wife's boots and rain gear—along
with a collection of large-scale maps which she reads
fairly adequately, much to her surprise.

I find in Scotland a land of stability and unchanging
timelessness—a quiet contrast from the ever-changing
whims of the world. And yet, just when all seems
familiar, it yields lovely discoveries. Moods change
from gray, soft-rain melancholy to sun-drenched bril-
liant landscapes—and back again in minutes. Even the
intrusion of man with the ritual spring burning of the
hill heather has an appropriate welcome aroma. The
friendly Scots' traditional farewell of "haste ye back"
has an emotional sincerity which has drawn us time
and again to return to the highlands.

54

Allegorical Realism—CONEY ISLAND
Egg tempera on gessoed masonite. 1949. 48″ × 36″
Collection: *Mr. & Mrs. Joseph M. Erdelac*

56

Representational Realism—LANCERS
Acrylic on gessoed masonite. 1968. 64″ × 48″
Collection: *Mr. & Mrs. Irwin Engelman*

I am "other realism"—not the magic kind. I have never been as interested in surface facts and natural appearances as I have been in creating truths that could only exist in the art. After a few lapses with oil in the dim past, my media (all water-base) have evolved from gouache, egg tempera and gelatine-size to acrylic over a thirty-year period.

To attain visual truths I render forms as they solidly exist in space — but without atmosphere. Water-base media do not lend themselves to atmospheric illusion as does oil paint. I usually arbitrarily employ a light source, cast shadow, reflected light, linear perspective, etc. My light source cannot be identified or measured. The cast shadow produced by the off-panel light is devised rather than being optically correct. While it may seem logical — a form that receives light from the left casts a shadow to the right — it is not accurate. The effect is optical rationality. The painting simply falls into the realm of reason. When I put this in sharp focus imagery the result is the containment of a definable, dimensional space. And it is the illusion of that space against solid objects that produces an awareness of reality. Essentially, what I paint is space, not objects. My purpose is to induce the observer to sense the truth of my reality rather than impose his reality on my visions. It hardly matters whether or not the observer likes what he sees as long as he is drawn into the illusion.

I have explored allegorical, symbolic and romantic realism among other things. These seem to have grown into an internal realism — a realism of the mind couched in familiar terms that give an appearance of external matters.

The scratchboard illustration I do for young adult books is a different matter. While these reflect a lifelong yen for uninterrupted form and the influence of those currents fundamental to my painting, they are restricted to greater or lesser degree by the printing press, marketing economics and a text for which they are adjuncts. These images are pictorial in that they offer clear-cut recognizable forms and shapes. They have selected light sources for the most part and, like my painting, they are arbitrarily devised. They are black and white and linear — however in reverse — there is a subtle schematic abstraction to them. Nature is not black and white. Gradations in nature are not crosshatched either. And surely, there exists in nature infinite value gradations — not just the five-to-ten value scheme I work in. These are graphic ideas — not rendered substitutions for actuality. They have dramatic intent aimed at enlivening specific literary content.

If I could pinpoint my creative arena, I should say that I was left of pure realism and right of pure abstraction, but never in the middle. I am a realist—the "other realist." But more than that, I like to think that artistically I am a humanist never outside the full range of reality's possibilities as those possibilities now exist, will exist or can exist within the human experience.

LEONARD EVERETT FISHER

Born: New York City
Studied: Heckscher Foundation, Art Students League, Brooklyn College, Yale University School of Art
Clients: Over 200 juvenile books (author of 30); designed several U.S. postage stamps
Awards: Pulitzer Prize, Citations A.I.G.A.; The American Library Assoc.; Connecticut League of Historical Societies; numerous painting prizes
Member: Society of Illustrators
Teaching: Dean, Academic Affairs, Paier School of Art, Hamden, Ct., lectures extensively

Symbolic Realism—JONAH
Gelatine size on laminated rag. 1964. 39″ × 39″
Collection: Mr. & Mrs. Peter R. Mack

Romantic Realism—SKY AND SUN
Acrylic on gessoed masonite. 1966. 36″ × 24″
Collection: the artist

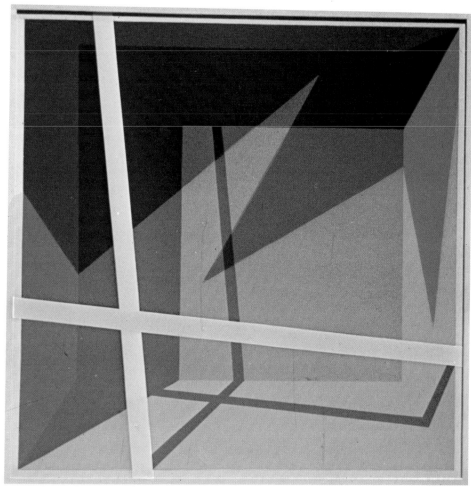

Dimensional Realism—SHADOW OF A RIBBON
Acrylic on gessoed masonite. 1970. 48″ × 48″
Collection: New Britain Museum

Representational Illustration—MOZART   59
Scratchboard. 1976. 18″ × 24″
Client: Kirsten-Artemis, Inc.

STANLEY W. GALLI

Born: San Francisco
Studied: S.F. Art Institute, Art Center School, L.A.
Clients: General magazines, children's books, advertising, wildlife painting, western paintings, postage stamps, sports magazines
Exhibited: New York, San Francisco, Rome, Los Angeles, Tacoma
Awards: Many
Member: San Francisco Society of Illustrators, Society of Illustrators, Society of Animal Artists
Teaching: San Francisco City College

Although I have illustrated for every conceivable project, my preference has always been to portray the outdoors, with emphasis on wildlife and the cowboy scene.

In the intense search-and-discovery mission that art seems to be, I have come to my own personal convictions about method. Mainly I strive to draw well—to learn the anatomy of everything, even the anatomy of a splash. My reasoning is that, with mastery of drawing, I can be in entire command of the picture space. Hard to do, and it takes forever. It is well worth the effort, though, because it is the only kind of accumulated savings that compounds in value and cannot be plundered.

My method of working is simple but laborious.

On an assignment I put very special effort in the conceptual stage. I feel that what I select to do for the particular publication, and its special audience, is the most important step. It requires a bit of analytical reasoning and a good amount of instinct. Often I go through reams of sketch paper trying to arrive at what I consider a clear pictorial statement for the assignment. The sketches to be submitted will all be worked out as accurately as my drawing ability will allow. If the drawings are accurate and convincing, I will have less problem in the finishing stage. There will be no areas of doubt and fumbling. The composition will be free of negative surprise that can destroy the rhythm of the composition.

When my sketches are accepted, I redraw the entire composition and transfer it to board or canvas. Areas that have been drawn with reasonable accuracy are polished up. In the case of wildlife drawings, my first sketches are close in character to the subject. Since there is still much I don't know about wildlife, I refer to my files, or field sketches, for specific animals or birds. It is rare to find views that I could use totally. It suffices to have the photo give me the nuances in the character of the subject. The photo plus accumulated knowledge helps in making a convincing picture. Often the zoo and aviaries are my reference. If I can photograph there, I do. If need be, I make rough clay models of the subject for lighting.

My western paintings go through much the same process as I've described above. With one exception: I often draw totally from memory with only casual reference to my files for details of gear and markings of horses. I have occasionally tried photographing a set-up but it never seems to work successfully for me. Somehow the photograph begins to dominate my thinking and I produce a stilted picture. I prefer acting out the scene on the drawing board and then use reference aids to arrive at a "ring of truth."

I will not linger on techniques; they seem very personal marks of each artist. I experiment widely with techniques and try to find ways of doing things that emphasize the picture content.

61

Stanley W Galli

Stanley W Galli

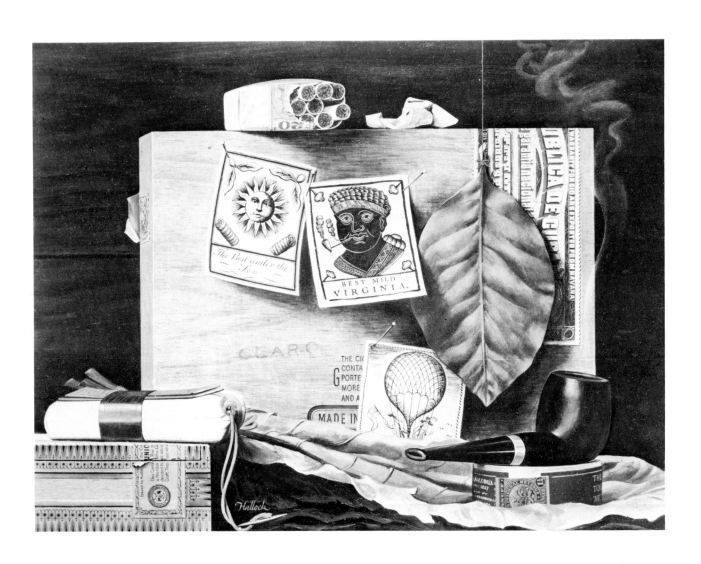

ROBERT HALLOCK

Born: Winchester, Mass.
Studied: Chouinard School of Art, L.A., Art Students League
Clients: Numerous advertising and publishing, SI Annuals 1,
   18, and 20 U.S. Postal Service, *Lithopinion* magazine
Awards: Art Directors', Society of Illustrators, C/A, New
   York State Award, AIGA, Society of Publication Designers,
   etc.
Member: Society of Illustrators

I have been an artist for many years but, for the past few, I have concentrated on a wide range of graphic design. (I founded and was art director and managing editor of *Lithopinion*, the quarterly graphic arts and public affairs journal, sponsored by Amalgamated Lithographers of America and the Metropolitan Lithographers Association, New York, from 1965 until 1975, when it ceased publication.) My career has encompassed many aspects of design, including still life painting similar to the examples shown here. All visual expression is based on design, of course — from postage stamps to murals, from packaging and typography to film making. I have done them all.

The most important part of design is getting a solid organization of the various ingredients involved. They must be properly balanced within the whole structure so that everything functions and nothing can be deleted. This is partly a matter of what "fits" the eye, and there are no easy rules for it. Research for a picture to establish authenticity often provides insight into the solution.

Realism in painting is essentially a romantic—even poetic—statement.

66

DONALD M. HEDIN

Born: Bridgeport, Ct.
Studied: Pratt Institute
Clients: Most major book publishers, magazines and
  advertising promotional work
Exhibited: Numerous galleries in Northeast; Salmagundi
  Club; Society of Illustrators; L.I. University
Awards: First Prize Conn. Arts Festival; Award of Excellence
  Society of Illustrators; Wm. Church Osborn Prize
  American Watercolor Society
Member: American Watercolor Society, Society of
  Illustrators

The demanding technique necessary for *trompe l'oeil* painting, which literally means "fool the eye," is so time-consuming that it doesn't appeal to everyone. However, to those who can thus lose themselves, it will produce rich results, and is well worth the effort.

In a true egg-tempera painting, the complexities and fragile qualities of that medium make for a small and dedicated group of artists to be greatly admired for their rare craftsmanship. However, the same general result can be obtained with acrylics and it is much easier. Because it has more body it can be pushed around more readily. One can drybrush, scumble or thin it to use in a pen!

This is the way my "tempera" acrylic painting is done: I apply myriad wispy strokes, many no larger than an eyelash, to produce a weave of color and tone. In various areas the strokes go in different directions, depending upon how I decide to handle the subject. The tiny strokes vary slightly in direction, to overlap, to weave a smooth pattern, somewhat like the scales on a fish. The direction, angle of the strokes, the shape, the type — straight, curved, longer, shorter, thicker, thinner — are all part of the mix. But the *individual* stroke should always be small enough to blend into the whole. On rounded forms the strokes may curve to follow the shape, altering slightly to crisscross each other. Warm colors over cool, light over dark. A little medium mixed in with the paint gives it a translucent quality, and modifies the colors slightly with each successive layer of paint. This, plus the use of transparent glazes, helps blend the tiny strokes. It also builds a color with depth and produces an effect not possible in any other way. No color applied in one application will give depth like one built up in this disciplined use of multiple glazes.*

Another aspect of the tempera technique that is achieved by this method is the smooth, even finish. No brush strokes show; textures are reproduced by *painting* the shapes of the material, be it rough bark, woodgrain, polished brass, woven cloth. Each little hole, bump of whatever shape that produces the eventual texture will have its own form, throw its own individual shadow, possess its own little highlight.

Tempera painting is not a quick technique. There can be no dramatic impasto treatments. It requires careful planning and execution.

*A glaze is a mixture of approximately 50% water, 50% acrylic medium, and a very small amount of color. Too much color will produce unwanted streaks, too little will have such meager results that you will need several coats. Experiment! I apply glazes with a flat sable brush, in smooth, unhurried horizontal strokes. Do not go back over the freshly-laid glaze. Do not hesitate in the middle of a stroke. Remember, each successive glaze will darken as well as modify the color.

From the book THE ART OF STILL LIFE PAINTING © 1972 M. Grumbacher, Inc.

69

70

DAVID KILMER

Born: Waterloo, Iowa
Studied: Wayne State College, Colorado Institute of Art,
  John Jellico, Dane Clark
Clients: Book jackets, posters and advertising
Exhibited: New York & Chicago galleries
Awards: Several
Member: Society of Illustrators

Good reference material is especially important to anyone working with tight realism. I seek it out diligently — either by shooting it or finding it elsewhere. And I look harder all the time; too many times in the past after I've finished a picture, I've come across better reference.

I'd like to dwell on one particular assignment for this book. It was done for the Testor Toy Corporation.

I began with good scrap and decided to make the picture approximately 15" across. With the aid of a grid, I penciled my sketch up and on to a sheet of blue-green matboard to give me a ready-made background color. I strive to make my pencil drawing as true and detailed as possible for I think it wise to solve as many problems as I can in pencil.

I have no contrived painting techniques that I'm conscious of. There is no simpler statement I can make than to state that I just go all out to make things as real as possible—to do so, I use any tool or media I can think of to gain this end. This Testor piece was done with a combination of acrylic, tempera and colored pencils. It was painted for the most part from dark to light. The colored pencils were used sparingly as a final touch in selected areas. And of course, I save the big moment— the highlights for last. That's when everything pops into place and seems finally realized.

CO-OP VILLAGE
AUXILIARY POLICE
CLASS OF '74

BIRNEY LETTICK

Born: New Haven
Studied: Yale School of Fine Art; Louis York; Deane Keller
Clients: Paramount Pictures; Columbia Pictures; Warner Bros.; Time, Inc.; Merck Pharmaceutical; Kodak; Coca Cola; Heublein; R. J. Reynolds; P. Lorillard; Sony, Avon Products, Hood Dairy Products, etc.
Exhibited: Brooklyn Museum, Yale, New Britain Museum of American Art, Albright Knox Museum, Graham Gallery, FAR Gallery
Awards: First Prize Bicentennial Coin Design for Conn., Gold Medal '63 Society of Illustrators
Teaching: Director of New Haven Art Workshop '46-'72

Many "sophisticates" shudder at the word "realism." To some people and many critics it is a lesser type of art, old hat, passé and academic. Realism is, however, the motive force in the development of art, the product of thought about life; it reflects the period. Critics have said that non-objectivism has cornered the market on the "art of painting," the turning point of coming of age. Be assured that this art is found in great realists' works. It is not so much a means in itself as it is a means to an end, a subtle sophistication on its way to expressing something.

Realism is the intellectual art which depicts such emotions as anguish, love, happiness, not only with symbols but with social experience. One does not "imitate" nature to achieve this. It is a *re-creation* of nature which makes for the best realism. The artist must have a background of much study and practice, with great knowledge of distortion and exaggeration of form, color and perspective in order to produce it, more than is found in most "modernist" paintings. Most of the latter dedicate themselves to the abstract, to the division of a flat space with interlocking geometric forms. The great realists, past and present, in a more masterful and complex way dedicate themselves to the same problems rooted in the real world. This takes unending study and love of nature.

"Why must you be a non-conformist like everybody else?" was a caption under an old *New Yorker* cartoon. A valid question regarding most of the non-objectivists today. But I must insist that non-conformity is a most important value to the realist. Without it he may be just another conservative. It's inborn, in my opinion, but one must know and study nature and understand the rules so that they can be manipulated as one chooses.

Good realism is not a matter of "aping" nature. It is rather an approximation of nature; the artist must exaggerate, know the subject, feel it, live it, know all its possibilities and use or eliminate them.

Illustrators often use photographs as an aid to producing a painting; very necessary with the impossible deadlines we all have. But one must know how to read a photo and to edit it. One sees best when one knows best and has a complete understanding of nature and anatomy and optics to be able to correct the camera's distortions.

Patronage of art by the Church during the Renaissance to that of big business today has nurtured great innovative painting. Art has always been demanding and competitive. It doesn't just "happen." It's a planned, intellectual product commissioned (by the gods) as always.

"Let the art happen" is a phrase one hears in many art schools. There's a lot more to it than that.

77

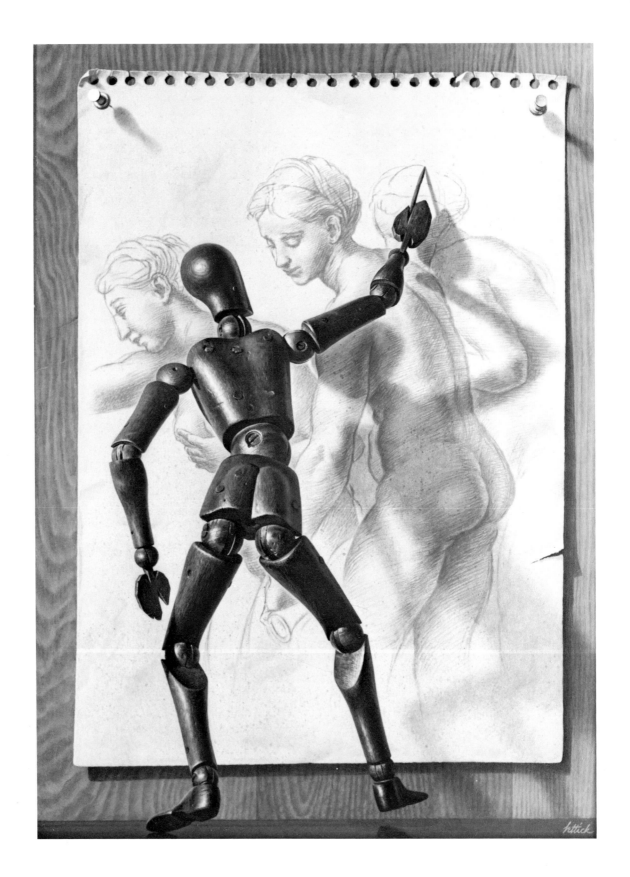

4" x 8" COLOR SKETCH IN OIL
FULL

3½" x 8" LIMITED COLOR SKETCH
IN ACRYLIC

THE BATTLE OF HASTINGS, small preliminary sketches

TOM LOVELL

Born: New York City
Studied: Syracuse University, H.V.B. Kline
Clients: National Geographic, True, Woman's Home
   Companion, Collier's, American, McCall's, Ladies Home
   Journal, Reader's Digest, Life, Good Housekeeping, etc.
Exhibited: National Cowboy Hall of Fame, McCulley
   Gallery
Awards: Prix de West, C.H.F. '74, Franklin Mint Western
   Portofolio '74, Society of Illustrators Hall of Fame '74
Member: Society of Illustrators

My approach to picture making begins with learning all I can about the subject through first-hand observation, if possible—e.g. visiting the site; then reading available material to provide historical background. The next step usually includes several small (post card size) very rough sketches for mood and general effect. In the case of the Battle of Hastings, preliminary research revealed that the site of the battle had so changed that visiting the spot would serve no purpose. The concentrated essence of the fight lay in the Norman Knights breaking like a wave against Harold's wall of shields, and a small thumb-nail rough confirmed this.

The next step was a charcoal drawing 13″ by 22″ in which design and action were established. Models were then photographed in action poses and the whole redrawn in a finished cartoon the outlines of which were transferred to a gesso panel. Before starting the final painting, several small color sketches were made in oil.

In this particular commission there existed one invaluable source of reference in the Bayeux Tapestry, made shortly after the invasion and miraculously preserved. This well-known creation shows armor, weapons, shield designs, etc. in stylized by useful array. No attempt was made to photograph horses in action. No real weapons or armor were available so home-made approximations were employed. A somewhat darkened foreground, as from a passing cloud-shadow, complemented by limited back-lighting accentuated the central areas and simplified the whole as much as possible. The selection of moment put the observer directly into the battle and at the same time provided the necessary center of interest in the dominant figure of Bishop Odo, and hinted at the final outcome.

As the eye moves over any given scene, sharp focus is lost and found, and I try for this effect in my painting. Put another way, I enjoy the use of detail, but I try to keep it subordinate to the more important demands of composition. In making a painting of this kind I am guided by two major considerations: one, that the presentation be made in a believable, you-are-there manner; two, that it fall into the strongest and simplest design commensurate with its required elements.

Charcoal sketch, 13" × 22" for THE BATTLE OF HASTINGS

Mooncraft of the Future

Because I've been engaged for 18 months in painting a 68-foot mural that rises six stories at one point, I find it difficult to talk about much else (or even to *remember* much else).

The mural is one of two (Eric Sloane's is the other) in the new National Air and Space Museum in Washington, D.C. Rather than talk about it myself, I'd like to quote from the *Airman* Magazine story on it.

ROBERT T. McCALL

Born: Columbus, Ohio
Studied: Columbus Fine Arts School
Clients: Most leading magazines, many advertisers and publishers, U.S. Postal Service
Exhibited: Extensively
Awards: Many
Member: Society of Illustrators

"The viewer 'reads' the space mural from the left where the painting begins at the beginning with the birth of the universe. In a cataclysmic burst of energy, the planets, stars and other wonders of the cosmos are born.

"Dominating the right third of the work is the triumphant figure of an American astronaut standing on the cratered surface of the moon holding an unfurled flag. A fellow astronaut stands behind him alongside the lunar rover. Space and landing craft are evident as is the earth.

"Imagery is the central focus of the upper portion of the mural, with the sun and cross-like shafts of light leading the viewer to look both up and out toward the future of mankind in space …

"He and his wife moved from Arizona to Washington when he began to paint actively.

"After putting together eight smaller studies, McCall finally worked out a complete ten-foot wide by ten-foot high model to work from. He drew two-inch square grids on the model that were later translated to one-foot squares on the wall canvas. The squares were numbered correspondingly.

"The painter worked from a complex scaffolding arrangement complete with nine levels of seven-foot planking that were connected by staircases. He physically moved the two-sectioned model from place to place and level to level during the eight-month painting job.

"He usually worked from 9 a.m. to 4:30 p.m. and through many weekends.

"The mural is painted with acrylics on primed Belgium linen canvas that is permanently bonded on the sheetrock wall.

"The artist was paid $75,000 by the Smithsonian for his painting.

"'But I'd have done it for nothing,' he said. 'This is true of all the really good things I've done.'

"'Of course, it's my biggest painting in size and significance. To an artist this is the greatest thing that can happen to him, to have something he's done viewed by a lot of people.'"

Before the mural (was there ever such a time?) my career went something like this: I was programmed to be especially interested in painting things that related to the military and to war because I grew up in that very impressionable period when a war was on.

I've painted promotional materials for such films as *2001: A Space Odyssey, Ice Station Zebra,* and *Tora! Tora!!*

I've free-lanced since 1958 and have been active in NASA's art program. My painting of the linkup between Apollo and Soyuz spacecraft last year was used on the cover of *Newsweek* and in several other publications.

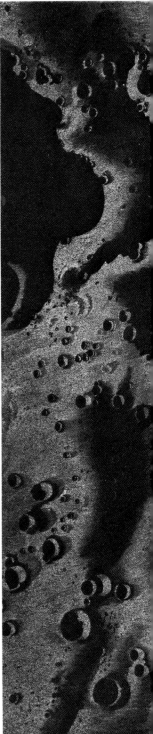

My background in traditional painting stems from study at the Art Students League under Frank Reilly. His course stressed the fundamentals — drawing and painting. During my last year of study I was on a half-day schedule so I was able also to work as quasi-apprentice to Dean Cornwell. Though I had no desire to imitate Mr. Cornwell's style, observing him at work was a most beneficial experience. His approval, when it came, was a great confidence-builder.

At the time I started free-lancing realistic painting

GERALD McCONNELL

Born: West Orange, N.J.
Studied: Art Students League
Clients: Major advertisers, publishers and trade books
Exhibited: Many private and corporate collections; U.S. Air Force Museum, Dayton; Patrick Air Force Museum, Florida; NASA Museum, Cape Kennedy; National Parks Department, Washington
Member: Trustee, Frank Reilly School of Art, Society of Illustrators, Founding Member of Graphic Artists Guild

was the usual approach. Fortunately, because of my training, I felt at ease with my earliest assignments.

Product rendering has never been my favorite form of expression. However, there is always need for this type of work and it is financially rewarding. The example I've included here was part of a campaign for Grey Advertising, which I worked on in conjunction with another New York illustrator, Howard Koslow, an expert in this area. Howard taught me a great deal about that handy tool, the airbrush. On this assignment I also did the lettering. It took me as long as the rest of the job. As in all product rendering, the idea was to make the pack and the cigarettes look better than they would have in photography. This can be achieved with modified perspective, elimination of unnecessary detail and adjustment of color values so they will appear cleaner and slicker in reproduction.

The dragon with the flower was a cover for *Bell* Magazine, published by A.T.&T. It was done with Designers colors and dyes. The three elements were selected by the art director to represent Red China. After gathering the reference material I made a detailed drawing of each object, establishing light and shadow patterns. I projected these onto doubleweight illustration board and painted the background dark, so that I could adjust all my values against it. I then painted both the dragon and the flower with dyes, which gave the brilliance I wanted. I did the final details with opaque colors.

The picture containing the F4C fighter plane was done from scrap gathered in England. I was there for the Air Force to visit several British and American air bases, in order to paint the F4C in action. This particular painting was of a small 16th century church situated at the end of one of the runways near Little Stukeley. It was ironic to note that the plane was already being phased out of use while the church would probably, if not destroyed by vibration, remain indefinitely. The 40″ high painting was done with opaque Designers colors.

The barn door and chain, one of my Sunday attempts at therapy, was a joy to do — no art director, no client — just myself to please. This was also painted with Designers colors on board. It's just a bit under life-size.

All my paintings in this manner begin with numerous pencil sketches with many design adjustments. When the final solution is reached, I transfer it to illustration board by use of a balopticon and do a very finished pencil drawing, which is then well fixed. I then cover the entire board with an overall tone which will set the color and mood of the painting. That done, I restate the larger areas with more opaque paint to the exact color and value needed, after which I proceed to the remaining areas, bringing the degree of finish up to my center of interest.

89

91

DONALD MOSS

Born: Somerville, Mass.
Studied: Vesper George School of Art, Boston Pratt Institute, Art Students League, Paul Rand, Will Burtin, Howard Trafton
Clients: Sports Illustrated, Time, World Books, advertising agencies and corporations, U. S. Postal Service, etc.
Exhibited: Westchester, Fire Island, A.I.G.A., Society of Illustrators, Art Directors, Katonah Gallery, etc.
Member: Society of Illustrators

During my art career, drawing and painting have been pure enjoyment, hard working and rewarding—in that order. My "bag" is sports as a participant and a fan from as far back as I can recall.

Growing up in New England, hockey was our winter sport and golf our summer avocation. After serving in the Marines, W.W. II, skiing and tennis took over in the spare times between working for art studios and publications. Thus, it was only natural that my paintings gradually became more and more sports-oriented. The "pure enjoyment" phase had started.

To illustrate, here are few examples from my Sports Illustrated assignments: "America's Best and Most Beautiful Golf Holes" — traveling from Cape Cod to Florida, Nashville to California to photograph and sketch for the final oils; "Lear Steam Race Car" — flying to Reno with Bill Lear in his private jet to render the first complete drawing of his secret racing machine; to Stowe, Vermont and Snowbird, Utah to ski with and photograph the U.S. Demonstration Ski Team; flying to Las Vegas to photograph the pro golf stars Nicklaus, Palmer and others for Surrealistic paintings to illustrate their putting for "The Deadly Stroke"; "Pointillist View of Houston's Champions" — a week at this beautiful golf course sketching eight key holes to depict, Seurat-style Impressionist paintings for a U.S. Open Golf story; the birth of a 12-meter, "Intrepid," sailing on Long Island Sound photographing the exciting America's Cup yachts with Olin Stephens, famed boat designer, for a step-by-step painting/collage assignment, and back to my first sport, hockey, photographing for a series of acrylic and oil paintings of Guy LaFleur and other top NHL stars of today's scene.

One of the most interesting assignments was to depict, in Surrealist fashion, the awesomely-difficult Oakmont Golf Course, north of Pittsburg. Seven of the critical holes, perfect subjects for Surrealistic paintings, were selected. Two are shown: the picturesque 15th hole, one of Sports Illustrated's "18 Best Golf Holes," and the final 18th, where a golfer might easily lose all perspective and view the golf ball as you see it here.

Painting sports has been and continues to be a kaleidoscope of variety, color and technical facility. It is enjoyable to have freedom of expression to fit styles to assignments whether they are high gloss enamels-on-Formica abstracts of "America's Ten Best Ski Runs" or the superrealism renderings of "The Guns of James Bond."

While "Magic Realism" has been the backbone of my earlier advertising art and some contemporary editorial work, I like to think that "Poetic Realism" is evidenced, certainly attempted, in current paintings and those being planned.

93

96

KENNETH RILEY

Born: Missouri
Studied: Kansas City Art Institute, Grand Central Art
   School, Art Students League, Thomas Hart Benton, Harvey
   Dunn
Clients: Magazines, books, paperback covers, advertising
Exhibited: Private galleries, National Academy of Western
   Art
Member: Society of Illustrators, National Academy of
   Western Art

I have always felt that picture making, whether for reproduction or gallery, carries the obligation to interest, excite and sometimes inform. With that as a premise the need seems to be to approach each picture as an individual problem with the solution made in terms of obligation to that particular problem and in the context of one's own method or means of expression. This, I think, tends to create a process of constant renewal for the artist as each picture becomes a new world to explore. The end product probably never completely comes up to the ideal vision, but the excitement is in the route traveled. This, I suppose, is why the probing quality of an artist's preliminary sketches is so fascinating, seeing one scribble among the many which may capture the whole spirit and form of what is later the finished idea.

I suppose the pictures I have enjoyed most doing have been those where a mood was involved. Something showing a specific point in time, usually with the human figure, and perhaps a particular type of light. We all respond to different stimuli in those things that go to make up style. I suppose these are some of mine.

HARRY J. SCHAARE

Born: Jamaica, N.Y.
Studied: N.Y.U. School of Architecture, Pratt Institute
Clients: Many books for leading publishers, ads for several
   motion picture companies and corporate publications
Exhibited: 11 galleries
Member: Society of Illustrators

In most of the illustration that I have done over the years, the subject matter has usually dictated the medium. For figure work I prefer casein; for portraits, oils; for landscapes, casein; and for seascapes, watercolor. When a job crosses the line of two of these subjects I combine mediums. In the water scenes I just use opaques for the figure work and detail, and watercolor for the sea and other areas. True, it is crossing mediums, but if the result works, why not? Some of the illustrations shown here were done in casein, some in combination, and the largest in a straight traditional watercolor. Lately, I have gotten into watercolor more and more and have developed some techniques that I shall explain.

Watercolor is often called one of the most difficult mediums to handle. This is probably so, because to acquire the desired spontaneity, softness and sparkling sharpness of whites of the traditional watercolor painting, very little or no opaques should be used. This means, of course, that a minimum of mistakes can be made in tones and values of large areas. In small and detailed sections some opaques may be sparingly used.

The key to a successful watercolor painting, I think, is planning. Working slowly and carefully. Planning the area to be painted with relation to tone and color is essential so the desired effect can be achieved on the first try. To help in this regard, areas to be kept white, or very light in color or tone, should be masked out with maskoid or rubber cement. After the background and other surrounding areas are completed, the masking should be removed leaving the sparkling white of the paper. If some of the edges of the white area are too sharp or stiff a clean typewriter eraser or sharp razor blade will soften them. Because of treatments like the above you should make it a habit to use only the best quality of watercolor paper or board.

The order in which the colors and tones are applied is another factor to be considered. Since you can only go from light to dark, the necessity for planning beforehand what colors, areas, and values, are to be done and in *what order* is essential.

There are many techniques that can produce endless effects. When working wet-in-wet, the softness and blending of washes can produce a quality almost impossible to acquire in other mediums. By controlling the moisture on the board and brush, many variations of this same effect are possible. An electric hair dryer is a fine tool to use to push water or to rapidly dry a tone for a desired quality. Also it helps control unplanned accidents of color movement.

Cotton swabs, tissues, blotters and sponges all have their uses—as has common table salt sprinkled in wet areas for great effect. Try it!

103

WILLIAM TEASON

Born: Kansas City, Mo.
Studied: Kansas City Art Institute
Clients: Dell, Popular, Fawcett, Berkley, movie posters, advertising
Exhibited: American Watercolor Society, National Academy of Design, Society of Illustrators
Awards: 1971 American Watercolor Society "High Winds" Award, 1975 American Watercolor Society Mario Cooper Award, Mystery Writers of America "Raven" & Scroll Award
Teaching: Art Center, Tenafly, N.J.

This acrylic painting was inspired by a seashell that reminded me of a Greek war helmet. I felt if it were placed on top of an antique drawing or an engraving of a Greek warrior, that something interesting might come out of it. I composed these on an old black trunk that, fortunately, I had in the basement. After a few trial sketches for composition and color, I photographed the still life. Then I went to the Metropolitan Museum of Art for shots of Greek heads.

Fine detail is of great interest to me so sharp photographs are invaluable. There are faults to be overcome with photos, too, of course; you must make changes and not be a slave to the photo. Do what you must to make a better picture. Change size relationships, contours, tonal effects.

I did the final drawing in pencil on tracing paper and transferred it to a ¼″ masonite panel to which four or five thin coats of acrylic gesso had been applied on both sides to prevent warping. I use India ink to darken transfer lines. Later I traced the head of the warrior separately. I then applied a wash of burnt sienna which gave me a warm underpainting and allowed the drawing to show through. With my props at hand, I blocked in all areas, using a matte medium and water. At this stage I *approximate* the color values. I start thinly and build up gradually to a desired effect (which I'm not certain of in the beginning). I believe that warm tones applied over cool tones and vice versa give good results. I have a tendency to arrive at the end result with the paint too thinly applied. I try to remind myself to overcome this fault. By more build-up, I don't mean that *all* areas should be thick—I prefer it varied. In any stage of acrylic painting the application of the paint can be opaque, semi-transparent, glazed, scumbled or scrubbed. At some point decisions must be made to head in a definite direction in color, intensity and grayness.

I used a Liquitex matte varnish for the final finish. The instructions say to use one thin coat, which I do. They're right. I like the effect. It's important to make sure that all areas are covered so that you end up with an even sheen over the entire painting.

Unlike many of the artists in this book, I have done very little illustration. My work has been described as "reality invested with images hauntingly suggestive, rather than visually explicit." Somehow I feel that my work *is* explicit, but somewhat like a story of Kafka's which explores in great dead-pan detail something which does not physically exist. One critic called me a "cinemaconologist" (i.e. one whose paintings look like scenes from films). This was meant to be an insult, but I took it as a compliment. As one fascinated with moving images and shifting planes of reality, I have made films influenced by my paintings, and paintings influenced by my films.

I have been told that my work has strong psychological overtones, and I guess it's true. Of course, I feel that daily life on this planet has strong psychological overtones, which I simply try to portray. I feel that I exaggerate about ten percent. This is enough to cause much of my work to be considered bizarre.

I work mostly in egg tempera, although recently I have been experimenting with acrylic. I have painted more nuns than anything else. I suppose I feel that the particular order I depict is the perfect fusion of a beautiful abstract shape and a spiritual anachronism, out of place in this Panglossian "best of all possible worlds." I have also painted a lot of bicycles. These give me some elegant abstract forms to work with (especially the shadows) and are often seen in positions of danger. Old walls and pavement fascinate me because they are full of Turneresque tones and shapes, working against what man tries to make of them.

In the past I used my own children as models, but they have all grown up now. Still (based on old drawings and photographs) I continue to paint them as they were. I have been working for years now on a picture of my daughter Carri, methodically filling in the shadows thrown by a single bicycle, which has been moved to different positions on the pavement until the white negative silhouettes fill the entire panel. The white design on the carpet and the pattern of light from the window fulfill a similar function in "The Parakeet" (reproduced here) where Carri seems to be imprisoned in her own world of intense stillness.

My son Sean in "The Corner Seat" stares at the viewer with the clarity of youth, while behind him hangs a huge ring with a single mysterious key. In "The Newborn Kitten" his large hands almost hide the form of the young newcomer. In the background the mother's gaze is distracted elsewhere.

In another work the young artist comes upon a manhole while drawing a chalk maze. He simply incorporates it into the design (sometimes as a face) and proceeds on his way. Eventually he will finish the labyrinth — and find himself imprisoned within it. Elsewhere, a young girl on a city street has just finished sketching a chalk flock of birds in frenzied flight. She has also just loosed a real bird from its cage to mingle (as seen from above) with the imaginary birds. The grooves in the concrete resemble the bars of the cage. One of the chalk birds seems to be *in* the cage. A pet kitten stands next to a chalk bird, watching the real bird with great intensity.

These are the things I like to paint.

ROBERT VICKREY

Born: New York City
Studied: Yale, Art Students League, Yale School of Fine Arts, Wesleyan University
Clients: *Redbook, Ladies' Home Journal, Esquire, McCall's, Look, Good Housekeeping,* Avon Publishers, etc.
Exhibited: Extensively. Represented in numerous public and private collections
Awards: Edwin Austin Abbey Mural Fellowship and Prize, American Artist Magazine Citation, Audubon Artists Award, American Watercolor Society Award, National Academy of Design, Florida Southern College, Hallmark Award, Jos. S. Isidor Gold Medal, etc.
Member: American Watercolor Society, Audubon Artists